two hands
one prayer
no words
but love

Sacred Love Poems

Colin Willcox

Also by Colin Willcox

70 poems on the ever present stillness when the quiet path of appreciation encounters the timeless soul of Nature.

Sacred Love Poems

ISBN: 978-0-9573136-0-6

Published by The Quiet Bell Press

iamcolin55@gmail.com
www.thequietbell.com

First Lines

23 The weather seems suspended
24 I know all the flowers by now
25 Tiger lilies, did I say
26 You are the softest thing I know
27 I remember everything you told me
28 Every bird knows the evening light
29 The sun knows how to do things
30 There are songs today hidden
31 At dusk the geese
32 Come into the rain with me
33 We know all the songs now
34 I long to build my prayers invincible
35 The moon tonight, crescent
36 I know what I should be saying
37 The silent path that beauty weaves
38 Two pigeons in this endless world
39 The soft quiet lady on the edge of the sun
40 Is this all it takes to remember
41 The deepest silence of night
42 There is only one path through the woods
43 The many eyes of beauty
44 Scented flowers
45 I realise now why the trees wait for me
46 I cannot sleep at night by thoughts

1

I wonder what my day will bring me
that I will find
most difficult
to love

I wonder what my night
will say
when I tell her
where I dimmed my light
and when
I forgot to pray

there is always one more reason
to love
one more moment
to forgive

and a million times a second
is not too often
to begin

2

The Earth sees herself through our eyes
dances our senses
to each new day's surprise
The rainbow of existence
says stay
stay You
stay delicately mindful
fragilely awake

For life is
life is as she is
never empty never full
but never too much
never too much beauty
never too much life
never too much love
to discover

3

I have counted all the ways
that light
touches everything
at dawn
one single source
and a thousand billion rays
of pure
undiluted
life
Everything lives in light
even darkness
has to admit it
and once started
fire
breeds
fire
and love
takes care of it

Light is like that
never ending
love
is always
just beginning

4

I used to once believe in love
falling
like darkness
into perpetual
light
before I could see
with pure eyes
and speak
with an undefeated
naked
heart
but now I know
the million shades of grey
that rise up from the dark
are all that I need
to illuminate
the world
Love is a choice
I heard you say
always ready
for giving
in very ordinary ways
Love is everything
we live for
every day

5

this is where the day begins
eyes open
and not even thought
distorts
the unnamed pattern
of light

awareness
and no centre
nothing
outside the circle
nothing
and everything
within

this is what we live for
discovering the timeless
in the moment
infinity
in the familiar
love
within the seemingly
unloved

6

There are moments of silence
this stillness is our home
where hunger is forgotten
where loving
          is grown
instances of seeing
that seek no other now
surges of being
such as sharing
          allows

Sometimes we allow this,
          the opening link to where we are
                              to who we are
                              to why we are

and sometimes it seems
our whole life is that worship
the awakening, the mystery of each other
Yet such dedication is never filled
for the collective spectrum of our being
is utterly irresistible
          to itself

7

In my mind, I carried words
woven into patterns
that my dreams believed
would speak
a language
enlightened
with love

I don't need words now
I can hear the evening birds
singing
the end of their day
and the apple trees here
show me
all their buds
preparing for the Spring

and I don't care how many words
would have to surrender
in these final minutes
of the fading light

until I speak once more
with the silence
of an overflowing
heart

8

So who are we
when we close our eyes
silent
silent
reflection

Who are we
in the stillness
that arises
when we so fully accept
that we have no answers
that even the questions
cease

this may be our secret
that the circle of awareness
begins
and begins
and begins
without end

words and names
have nothing new to tell us

only silence
can pronounce
our presence

9

I love the ordinariness of days
waking
and even before the waking
some half-remembered glimpse
of this soul thing
washed in secret dreams

All the tiny fragments of time
pearled together
all the senses
awake awake

and one by one the thoughts come
to remind me
how precious
this stillness
speaks

A whole day to fulfil
everything
to be discovered
surrounded
by nothing
but light
and shadows
of light

10

the leaves of time
lie scattered in the dark
and all the flower buds I have
close their colours
and hide their eyes
the birds are here
but silent
the moon
and all the planets
disappear
yet there is one light
we believe in
that lives
beneath the surface
of the sun
one light
stronger
than anything
all the worlds of darkness
could destroy
one light
burning to remember
whatever
we do
for love

11

the grass this morning
wet
and the way the mist
caresses
the shape of trees
surrounds me
with grace

this is the only breathing
that matters
the leaves
and the touch
and the sighs

this is where
the darkness breaks
the spell
of silence
(you left)

and yet
it's just another dawn
waiting
for something
(like this)
to begin

12

The great white bird of heaven
has opened
her innermost wings
She knows
that flight
is not forever
and that darkness comes
just after
the sweetest note
the wild birds sing

Such sleep
is like an angel
in my heart
whispering your absence

and waking to the dawn
a blackbird
or something just as bright
catches me
gliding
eyes open
into your blinding
compelling
web of light

13

Do you remember the morning
my lord
swallows leaving
and the whole damn sky
quiet with light

Was this planned
these trees
my early footsteps
a cat
waiting by the wall

Days are always holy in the mind
sacred to body
touched
and kind

Yes, we begin again
we begin
again
our new day begins

and we recognise
our perfect place
continues to
surround us

14

The world at last
grows quiet
to my touch
where once only the night
and your silent
breathing
were enough
The darkness
that I thought
was outside
is sleeping
in your eyes
and not even the moon
moves
across
your unlit sky

I listen to the owl
that is tempting you
awake
and these wings
that brush against your face
is all that you'll remember
as my hand
takes their place

15

This is what is true

today
is here to stay

everything
is exactly
in place

anything can happen
and be welcomed
within

this is all that love is
the freedom
to be
face to face
with what is

16

I never grow used to this
the evening mist
when the moon breaks through

I don't care how many times I've kissed
the spaces you left me
to complete
I want to line up all my promises
like soldiers
to protect you

and these clouds tonight
will be my witness
and the darkness
coming
will be my seal

The silhouetted trees
is where I miss you
whenever something beautiful
illuminates my mind

The universe is growing
within everything
we are

17

there are cycles within the seasons of being
    there are gifts you leave me
            of feelings of Spring
there is newness flowering your nearness to me
    and I am still amazed
    and don't know how to say it
    in words you do not know

Sometimes the river flows backwards to meet me
'Here I am' whispers life all over again
'So this is where you live' comes the rain
    and I listen to the distance
            exploding inwards
    and I turn to each direction
            and I am with you
            and our little star
                    is so alive today

I feel greenness and growing
            moving very still
I touch the morning open
but I don't know what to do with such beauty
Creation takes my hand
and answers very softly
'I love you'
just when I was wondering
what I should do next

18

Every day begins like this
life opens her wings
to include us completely
and one by one
the angels bring us
their most precious gifts
to forgive

This is the deepest secret we know
that everything that most needs
our loving
is wrapped
in unloved disguise

and anything we choose to love
becomes beautiful
to our eyes

So many opportunities
to create
this earthly paradise

so many circles
and only
one centre

19

I remember your eyes now
quiet
as the full moon
pressed
against my darkest
star lit
sky

and I feel your breathing move
a thousand galaxies of mine
into place
to where the sun
can find me

yet at night
in the dark
all alone
the light
that my closed eyes
most listen for
is your soft hand
brushing aside
the distance
and resting
like a nest
within my own

20

The birds don't die
do they
when winter nights
become too much darkness
to bear
yet even summer days can be so long
for tired wings
and unsung prayers

Promise me this
Whatever kind of day you live in
you will continue
to ignore
all the ways
that love
can so easily
be forgotten

Memory is like the trees
and every season
has its dreams
to compare
but love
has only one voice
and nothing but itself
to repair

21

I am watching the sky for some sign of you
and my fingers will touch anything near
in case
some texture
some colour
some smoothness
may betray
a memory of skin
still looking
for something to kiss

I am waiting for this to begin
the long journey to love
never knowing
that time
is nothing to believe in
and that everything
ends like this
expanded
beyond recognition
but exactly
the same

Seagulls are so beautiful
going home
together

22

It's not as easy as it seems
waiting for the sun
in the rain
in the dark
whilst outside
the dancing world
makes sweet promises to the heart
that no one notices
never come to pass

I am still praying for the rain
to remember me
but I know that it is true
that when the water comes
to tempt my roots
that I'll be spiralling upwards
to look for you

and these fallen feathers
that I offer you
are everything
they are meant to be

wings are always paired
with sweet desire
(so that love
does not fall apart
when romance
catches fire)

23

The weather seems suspended
in her winter waiting
and I can sense the wings of time
are ready with their secrets
and surprises

That special beauty of being
unfolds
just as surely as the weather
plays cold
but I discover places I can stand in
people
and moments
that make it easy

and such a moment
such a place
such a one

is always near

24

I know all the flowers by now
the clumps
the clusters
the solitary stem
the palest colours
the brightest
smoothest
softest
sweetest
and the bent one
dusty from the rain
that sleeps now
watered
in my blue jar
rescued from life
to resurrect
love's fire

I have learnt that flowers are as sensitive
as time is
and days that I waste
without you
may blossom without me
as petals fall
so beautifully
out of reach

25

Tiger lilies, did I say
or fire
caught up in flames
or succulent fruit
in ripest season
juiced
or kisses
for any reason
that can be imagined
or induced
or forgiven
or silence
as the deepest well
the waiting
empty well
that echoes
every whisper
of Heaven
of Hell

Look a little higher, my darling
the light
the rain
the sky

and all around you
the Earth
is here

26

you are the softest thing
                    I know
your lips

and riding the contours of your skin
is like rain
on a thirsty day in June

I know petals just as soft
and your eyes
      were they wings
would pass the clouds
      and glide
like sunlight in the mist
      touching everything
            naked
                  with love

27

I remember every word you told me
about angels
waiting for the moment
of doubt
to pass

and with your ring
you drew a circle
and etched
both our names
within one heart

and then you turned the glass
face to face
the moon
our eyes
were one

You know the truth
light
is always present
in this world
nothing
is unreflecting
when we remove
our masks

28

Every bird knows
the evening light
comes to pass
and sleeping soon on silent trees
is everything they need
to believe in

I used to believe in darkness
enfolding night
maybe a few stars
to follow
and a single moon
to count time with

but now the long days
never end
without you
and my bed is so far beneath the trees
that even if I could catch you
falling
open winged
you would be the rain
pressed against my face
and your feathers would be
the thousand touches
of sleep

29

The sun knows how to do things
day by day
light upon the world
and everything grows
warmer
and alive
Sometimes we live in orbits
spinning around each other
balanced
connected
but never touching
I want to land
on every planet
that you feed on
be the light
to encircle love
within your reach
(this is all the sun does
reminds us
to believe)
and you
do you turn towards me
or are you just
spinning past
in flight

30

there are songs today hidden
in the frosted grass
upon this path I travel

and the voices that I seek
to whisper me
awake to all their beauty
echoed in the trees
that faithfully
surround me
this is how my footsteps
find me
until even I forget
where I have been

all the sorrows of the past are melted
by one loved touch
and one shared dream

Oh look a flock of birds flash silver
catching sunlight
against a steel blue sky

and I can feel the evening in my body
the way the light is always
so perfectly with you

31

at dusk the geese
and the wild wild red
    of berries
        burnt by Autumn
the quiet river
two swans
    perfectly at home

silhouetted birds
    pooling their solitude
    in the sanctuary
        of familiar trees

and you
overflowing with the beauty
        of this world
            press close
    your eyes
        alive
        with awakened love

32

Come into the rain with me
Your hair
wet against your face
tells me everything
your closed eyes
speak to me of love
again
I don't know where you live
when your heart
dreams of home
but I want you to know
this world we live in
is everything
we can make it
and every day love
is all there is
to discover
fire and light
uncover beauty
in all the places
that need it
and it seems that you
wherever you are
must be the one
to reveal it

33

We know all the songs now
waterfalls at dawn
between the days
that we began to explore

all the songs
that the birds taught us
were more important
than time lost
in unforgotten regret

For the sun
little darling
knows nothing
of this darkness
and closeness
and presence
we miss

and nothing that we choose to say
can ever be compared
to a rainy
sunlit
unfenced sky
to watch the world
awake

34

I long to build my prayers
invincible
to anything
but love

yet sometimes
I forget
to close my eyes
(to God)
and in that instant
I want everything
to be perfect
and unchanged

There is still a kind of treason
that lingers in my desire
to unite
what can never be apart

and the only forgiveness
that is true
to this world
is to love
nothing
less
and everything
more

35

The moon tonight
crescent
and my eyes notice
only the distance
between the stars

Time is my only companion
and even the silence
whispering your name
knows that all the words I gather
in pretty shapes and sounds
lie
in broken lines
and speak
in unfamiliar tongues
to no one
but the dark

It is the language of the heart
I listen to
dancing in the shadows
you know
the way
the stars
pretend
to fade
by day

36

I know what I should be saying
to my angels
and to God

I know what the clouds must long for
when the empty rivers
pray

I know all the signs are facing
the only way
I can betray
anything
but the truth

I want this marked
on every moment
that I have blamed
for my absence
of faith
Life is
forgiving
and forever

Everything
is important
to love

37

The silent path
that beauty weaves
across the fields of time
sometimes branches
through the heart
or straight on
to chase the mind

We all stand there
every second comparing
life's golden promise
to one more leap of faith
It is so easy to believe
in other lives
ever seeking
something more beautiful
more perfect
more deserving
to love
and miss this dazzling world
tugging at our senses
here today
choose love
is what this life
wants to say
choose love
choose happiness
choose play

38

Two pigeons
in this endless wide world
a thousand miles of sky
and yet they choose this tree
this branch
leaves turning gold

Such companionship is rare
in human hearts, to sit so close
so connected
in a shared and steady silence

Nothing can describe
the illuminated moment
we notice we are not alone

39

the soft quiet lady
on the edge of the sun
leaned over to touch
what time had once begun

with clear eyes of silence
the moment stood still
and the orange light of evening
promised
it always will

now with life in motion
darkness comes to sleep
and that which wakes tomorrow
is what the angels of love
will keep

40

Is this all it takes to remember
your open hand
waiting
somewhere near my own
and your eyes
shining your beauty
or your voice
drawing me home
There is so much more
to everything you say
and only one journey
worth beginning
spiralled
tightly
around your heart
and glowing
upwards
to your lips
and downwards
encompassing
every
naked
colour
of bliss
that can forever
be obeyed

41

the deepest quiet of night
awakes me
to the memory of you
all the stars are darkened
when I close my eyes
the sleeping trees
are dreaming
and even my heartbeat
is listening
for you

Sometimes my whole world is empty
even colours hide
my thoughts know
there is no escape
that does not involve
surrendering
what I do not have
in order to see
what is truly mine
and tonight
it is you
that slips through my fingers
breathing
your distance
awake

42

There is only one path through the woods these days
leading
deeper
to the purest
brightest
rarest
pearl
you live
naked
as the silent
whisper
of your skin
you open
every jewel
of light
a thousand
galaxies
converge
whenever our darkest paths
divinely
merge

43

the many eyes of beauty wait
for the song of silence
to begin
the stage is set
the curtains rise
a single light
illuminates the world
and all the kaleidoscope
of colours
are alive

this is what we have come for
this unexpected dance
a million pieces of the day
held together
perfectly in place

and look   here we are
everywhere reflected
in never ending
play

44

The scented flowers
the multitude of leaves
the soft kiss of sunlight
upon your cheek

Nothing that we thought we needed
managed to survive
the surprise of Winter

Where once the forest cloaked us
in muffled shade and wild bird wings
we dance surrounded
by naked limbs
where silence swims
its spacious
waiting
song

beyond the words
we are at one
with the only love
that matters

45

I realise now why the trees
wait for me
every morning
why the grass is wet
like tears
before dawn

I have come to count
on that light
and the birds I know
wake with me
at the ending
of the night

I still look for you
in all the silenced moments
that catch me
totally aware
I lay a place for you
within my world
and note everything
you would share

the colours come to life
in your eyes
were you here

46

I cannot sleep at night by thoughts
of where my hand
might keep you warm
your neck
your breast
your waist
your thigh
Not even the scent
of your outstretched skin
can drown
the dissolving
spiralling
unspoken sound
your silent lips might betray
and the touch
of your half-closed eyes
dreaming
as they find their way
cell by tiny cell
unwrapped
maybe naked they explore
your golden
glowing
warming
burning
engulfing inner core
of pure
unblinded light

47

In my heart all these stars are sleeping
and the moon is waiting
for another day
to begin

This is the cycle of being
one moment at a time
and all the sweet memories
of our future
are true
and all the dreams
we will weave
into our waking past
are longing
to be believed

Light is always
timeless
and eyes contain everything
we notice
I notice you
a thousand miles
in every direction
is where you live
leaf by leaf our world finds us
facing each other's
absolute perfection

48

there are clouds tonight
and yesterday the snow came in
        suddenly
like remembering
        what is really important

there is no final leap
however carefully planned
the moment grows
slows down
expands

how many times this happens
        unnoticed
even listening
has borders
        we do not cross

Whatever else is promised
I find no higher goal
than to fully fuse
my many roles
        into one
                illuminating
                        sound

49

the sun this morning told me
everything I wanted
to be here
was coming
with the light
that I asked for

and now the colours are opening up
one by one
they hold me
in their broken arms

Somewhere in the reds
I touched you
and orange
you answered
with your yellow robe
and your green and blue
will always find me
indigo
to melt my violet heart
into the light
our souls
will never tear apart

50

Love does not hide
in our senses
Beauty is alive
when touched
by anything
as soft
as your soft
eyes

I do not forget you
when you close your eyes
we are not alone
are we
when we include the world

Life is everything
you think it is
so beautiful
you shape
this world

Yes we can live in heaven
when we totally
embrace this Earth
undivided
love
has no where else to go

51

I don't need more words
to hear the Robin sing
his early morning awakening

I don't need more thoughts
to see the oak tree
cloaked in leaves
dancing in the breeze

I don't need more names
for the flowers
surrendered
open petalled to the light

I don't need more distance
to discover the wonder
of where I am right now

I don't need to find
another object
moment, idea, person or place
more perfect
more deserving
to love

I don't need more time
to appreciate
every texture and dimension
of this borrowed life

52

The last time
the morning looked
so perfect
three birds were flying
that way
and all these trees
were just as quiet
just as real

there they are
the birds are still circling
and around me
every leaf in place
the world does not appear
to move
only clouds
changing shape

However deep the silence
the listener
stays the same

53

I love this season thing
the trees
and even the daffodils
renew their promise

Soon
every little bird
that sings your name
when weary
will settle in your branches
feathered in your warmth

and the deer
drinking from the pool
where once you swam
reflecting half of heaven
naked
and open
to the kisses
of the endless moon
the dawn you hid from
has returned
a million stars are traded
for a solitary
all-encompassing
infinite
delight

54

the time of rain is over now
the clouds have grown dry of despair
the rivers of time are still swollen
with all of the past
that we cannot repair

One sun, one day
is as much as I can hold
whilst at night
a sky full of stars
never quite know the way
my eyes
keep looking
for you

And something else
that I may not have mentioned
the breezes
and the ocean waves
seem somehow
to have learnt your name

At last I know where to find you
the thousand scents
of paradise
are wrapped
in the silken folds
of your absent kiss

55

I shall be the witness
to your truth
whenever
the shadows
outshine the sun

I shall keep the memory of you
burning
in all the abandoned places
that you outgrew
and I shall still be
present
in every direction
that you dare not
choose

I know that love
does not feed alone
and my hunger
is the whole world
every minute
spinning further
into the spiral
of your
awakening
heart

56

Know that there is no love
  that is not thunder
No thought
  that is not power
No dream
  that cannot flower
Nothing is ever wasted
No day is ever gone
You must come and realise
  the magic of it all
You can create your heaven
  for there is no hell, only walls
  between you and your richness
    your uniqueness in it all

Yet how can we grasp wild truth
  with a furrowed brow?
Answers are clothed in kindness
  and hint at soft content
The path is featherlight, and starlit
  reflected in our dreams
  curtained against darkness
  cushioned against falls
Contained within each minute
  is the answer to it all
Every little drop, every inch is new
  part of the ocean, the infinite
    the love that you grew
Every moment is your own
The answer that you're seeking
    is endlessly
        seeking you

57

and when our senses touch
merge
kisses
become spirals
of the soul

you are spread like light
upon an open world

lips
and all the secret shadows
you unfold
surrender

one ripple
a thousand centres
expand
explode
light
becomes light
and love
becomes love

58

I notice you in Winter
stretched
between the fingers
of these snow flakes
melting
in my empty hand
and out of the silences
you whisper me
like honey
sinking
into a dreaming sea

All the fragrances
your Earth
reveals me
your delights
are coded
in every breath
and depth
of life

This is how I remember you
second by second by second
living
in your exquisite world

59

The lady lies with folded wings
Deep asleep, and dreams
Trickle through the streams
Of the life to which she clings

It seems she struggles
In darkened contours
With unseen forces
That chase and drain
Her hidden stores

She's torn between
What the past has been
And the future's gleam and lures

Wild and maybe naked
Like a child, she could make it
Take it deep within the limits
Of her senses and her minutes

Life grows as she builds it
Now that she's strong enough to give it
She knows that she must live it
In the present that time lends her
And for each moment, surrender
To the magic living sends her

60

I stand at the very edge of you
and dip my fingers
in your trembling surface

wet

I watch the whirlpool spiral
downwards
inwards
endless
spin
from the depths
to deeper
timelessness
surrendering
to bliss
I sense you
sliding
falling
drop by drop
into
your liquid life
anywhere we touch
like water next to water
you melt me
into us

61

At this time of evening
the birds
choose their night
and my thoughts
carry you
into my deepest silence
where you sing
your presence

Life includes you
on purpose
Anywhere you live will do
all the earthly beauty
that love alone
can find
is always here
in your awakened eyes
and in your waiting hand

You are so beautiful in this world
you are everything
that lives
a million galaxies of time
in one
irresistible
totally surrendered
divinely chosen plan

62

the sky little darling
catches every raindrop in my heart
and water that I thought was mine
overflows
every time
the sun pretends dark

Through this day-to-day disguise
we think of as existence
I look for you
in even the most unlikely places
and find
that every moment is alive
with you
and nothing is left
unsaid
by your burning lips
and your unkissed breathing

I know you are the one
to constantly remind me
by your presence
and your glance
to look love
in the eyes

63

I am listening for the words
the night might use
to cradle you
to sleep
and the morning
sweet angel of light
what would she whisper
to enchant
your waking eyes
as the dreamy days of summer wrap
one more moment
for you to kiss

It is this endless
timeless
unknowingness
that promises
nothing more
and nothing less

than this
this
and this

64

one day all this fruit will pass

and memories that summer warmed
        and flowers
                busied by the bees

        one day
                soon

and words of love
                we did not speak
        mornings
                unnoticed
        and meetings
                we did not keep
evening songs
                forgotten
        grassy hills
                we did not reach

        one day

65

this used to be so simple
waiting for the flowers to bloom
and watching the way
the petals would fall
along your cheek
in the park somewhere
the hand you reach
to dismiss your hair
would suddenly
be the liquid sunset
I have watched for
It may be easier to believe
in butterflies
or still rivers on quiet evenings
or the sudden rush we feel
as the sun breaks free
from some golden cloud at dusk
yet the whisper of your eyes
never suspects
that this is just a reflection
and the hair that you unwind
is one of those rivers
tumbling through my mind
in repeated perfection
The clouds tonight
are those you left
to shade the moonlight
from your winter limbs

66

The angels of time
have grown quiet
again
and I need only your nearness
to remind me
why everything
has to change
(into love)

I remember the tree where I kissed you
with the light
of a thousand leaves
dancing in your eyes

now any tree will do
even one leaf
in your open palm
can shelter me
from the dark

One golden light
of dawn
and every single star
closes
her eyes
of night

67

The songs today
are those dripping from the leaves
outside this window
and the soft silent mist
is so often
in my thoughts
on days like this

Whatever else the morning does
the shape of trees
has found me
perfectly awake
to new meanings
of life

thank you
for the stream of prayer
my thoughts
create
of God

68

Here we are alive alive
one more moment to touch awake

This is what we'll miss:

the shape of things

the way that everything fits

moving from place to place
          yet never leaving where we are

time to be
     noticing the patterns
     how each day each minute begins anew

breathing in the world
     each breath the only one that matters

listening to the silence
     and all the sounds that sing
               their own vibration

realising that love has no dimension
     and nothing to contain or limit its end

here we are
one day or a hundred years no difference

There is so much more to love
               when everything is included

69

The evening of today
shakes its leaves
in breezes turning gold

the flowers of my life
have closed for the night
and not even moonlight
touches eyes
with such beauty
Yes I listen
and more delicate senses
watch me listen
for it is the moment of changes
and trusting the dark
the wings of the soul
enfold
ten thousand times
the sun

We are all connected
There is nowhere to go
but to the centre of the centre
of the beginning
of light

our Creator
who is all around us
within this holy creation
your vision unfolds
in the world today
when we see our Earth as heavenly

our everyday experience
is our spiritual exercise
and we forgive ourselves
and all others
by realising a greater truth

the path to pure joy is narrow
illuminated by love
beauty and compassion
in every moment and place
infinite
eternal

so be it